100 Hymns for Trumpet and Guitar

With Suggested Chordal Accompaniment

By William Bay

WILLIAM BAY**MUSIC**

Distributed by Mel Bay Publications, Inc.

WWW.MELBAY.COM

Index of Hymns

Title	Page

Title	Page

Preface

This is a collection of 100 of my favorite hymns arranged for trumpet solo. I have written suggested chordal accompaniment for each hymn so that a guitar or any chordal instrument can accompany the solos. Where appropriate, capo chords are shown. I have also indicated whether the guitarist should play fingerstyle or use a strum type accompaniment.

The music in this book spans centuries and represents a wonderful assortment of solos which may be used as preludes or offertories throughout the various seasons in the church year. This series also includes a separate volume for the Christmas season.

I have played many of these arrangements and feel that they can add much to any worship service. There is something very captivating about the sound of the trumpet in worship. I hope these arrangements capture that special sound for you as you play them.

William Bay

A Mighty Fortress is Our God
Ein' Feste Burg

Strum Guitar Acc.

Martin Luther
arr. by William Bay

Boldly ♩ = 90

Abide with Me
Eventide

Fingerstyle Guitar Acc.

Guitar: Capo 3rd Fret and Play Chords in Parentheses

William Henry Monk
arr. by William Bay

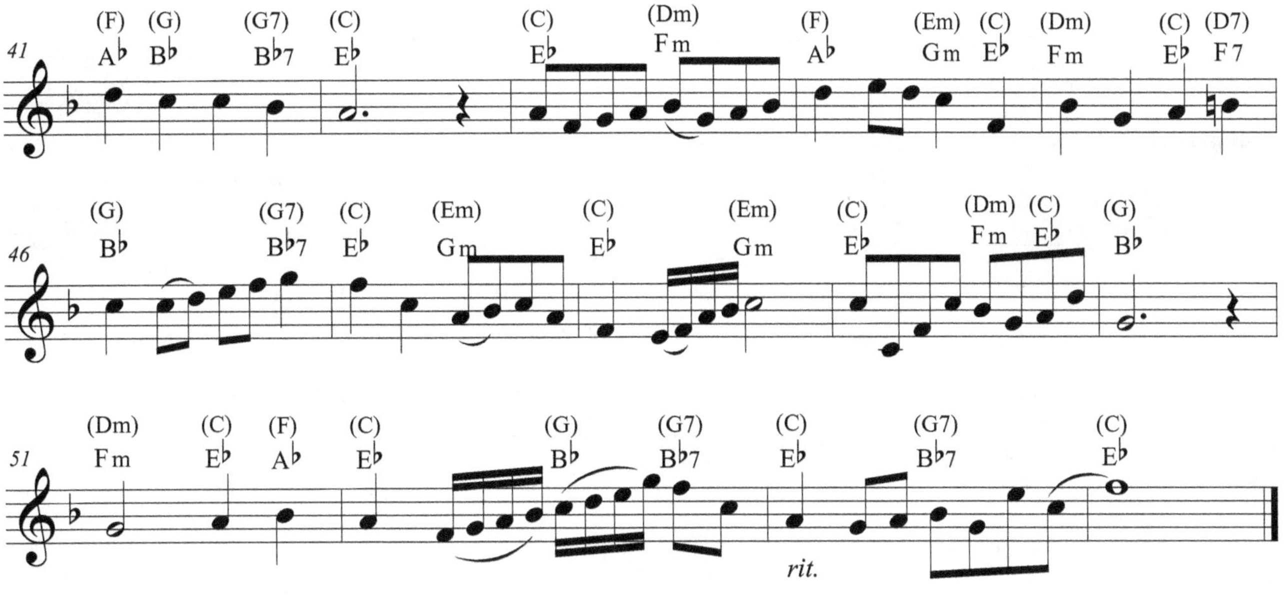
41
(F) (G) (G7) (C) (C) (Dm) (F) (Em) (C) (Dm) (C) (D7)
A♭ B♭ B♭7 E♭ E♭ Fm A♭ Gm E♭ Fm E♭ F7
46
(G) (G7) (C) (Em) (C) (Em) (C) (Dm) (C) (G)
B♭ B♭7 E♭ Gm E♭ Gm E♭ Fm E♭ B♭
51
(Dm) (C) (F) (C) (G) (G7) (C) (G7) (C)
Fm E♭ A♭ E♭ B♭ B♭7 E♭ B♭7 E♭
rit.

Adoro Devote

Guitar: Capo 3rd Fret and Play Chords in Parentheses

13th Century Plainsong
arr. by William Bay

Fingerstyle Guitar Acc.

8

Ah, Holy Jesus, How Have You Offended
Herzliebster Jesu

Johann Crüger
arr. by William Bay

9

All Creatures of our God and King
Lasst Uns Erfreuen

Guitar: Capo 3rd Fret and Play Chords in Parentheses

Strum Guitar Acc.

Geistliche Kirchengesänge

arr. by William Bay

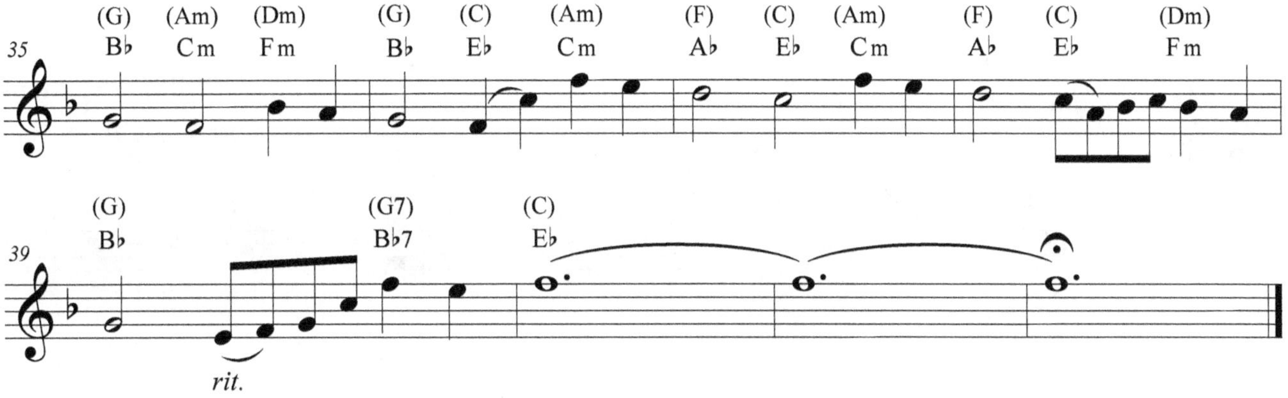
35
(G) (Am) (Dm) (G) (C) (Am) (F) (C) (Am) (F) (C) (Dm)
B♭ Cm Fm B♭ E♭ Cm A♭ E♭ Cm A♭ E♭ Fm
39
(G) (G7) (C)
B♭ B♭7 E♭
rit.

All Glory, Laud, and Honor
St. Theodulph

William H. Monk
arr. by William Bay

Strum Guitar Acc.

Boldly ♩ = 116

All Hail the Power of Jesus' Name
Coronation

All Praise to You, My God This Night
Tallis Canon

Fingerstyle Guitar Acc.

Thomas Tallis

arr. by William Bay

This page has been left blank to avoid an awkward page turn.

Alleluia! Sing to Jesus
Hyfrydol

Fingerstyle or Strum Guitar Acc.

Rowland Hugh Prichard
arr. by William Bay

Allegro ♩ = 130

60
D G Bm Em D G Bm Em
67
Am D7 G Em D G Dsus D7 G
74
Am G D G C G Em
81
D D7 G C D7 C G

Am I Born to Die?
Idumea

Guitar: Capo 3rd Fret and Play Chords in Parentheses

Fingerstyle Guitar Acc.

Sacred Harp, 1835
arr. by William Bay

Moderately (♩=118)

And am I born to die?
To lay this body down?
And must my trembling spirit fly
Into a world unknown!

And Can It Be
Sagina

Strum Guitar Acc.

Joyfully (♩=100)

Thomas Campbell
arr. by William Bay

51
Bm E7 A Bm E A E B7 E
57
A E A E D A E
63
A E7 A E A D B7 E
69
A D E A E A
rit.
75
E7 A D A Bm A E7 A

Be Thou My Vision
Slane

Guitar: Capo 3rd Fret and Play Chords in Parentheses

Fingerstyle Guitar Acc.

Traditional Irish
arr. by William Bay

Moderately ♩ = 104

22

Beneath the Cross of Jesus
St. Christopher

Guitar: Capo 3rd Fret and Play Chords in Parentheses

Frederick C. Maker

arr. by William Bay

Fingerstyle Guitar Acc.

Moderately ♩ = 96

23

Bread of the World
Eucharistic Hymn

Guitar: Capo 3rd Fret and Play Chords in Parentheses

John S. B. Hodges, 1868

arr. by William Bay

Fingerstyle Guitar Acc.

Breathe on Me, Breath of God
Trentham

Guitar: Capo 3rd Fret and Play Chords in Parentheses

Fingerstyle Guitar Acc.

Robert Jackson
arr. by William Bay

Christ Be in My Heart
Bi a 'Iosa im Chroise

Guitar: Capo 3rd Fret and Play Chords in Parentheses

Strum or Fingerstyle Guitar Acc.

Traditional Irish
arr. by William Bay

Slowly ♩ = 82

Christ Is Made the Sure Foundation
Westminster Abbey

Strum Guitar Acc.

Henry Purcell
arr. by William Bay

Boldly ♩ = 114

Christ the Lord Has Risen Today
Easter Hymn

Strum Guitar Acc.

Lyra Davidica, 1708
arr. by William Bay

Triumphantly ♩ = 106

Come Ye Faithful, Raise the Strain
St. Kevin

Fingerstyle or Strum Guitar Acc.

Arthur S. Sullivan
arr. by William Bay

Come Ye Sinners, Poor and Wretched
Beach Spring

Guitar: Capo 3rd Fret and Play Chords in Parentheses

Strum or Fingerstyle Guitar Acc.

Sacred Harp, 1835
arr. by William Bay

Come, Christians, Join to Sing
Madrid

Strum Guitar Acc.

Spanish Melody
arr. by William Bay

Come, Holy Spirit
Abbeville

Guitar: Capo 3rd Fret and Play Chords in Parentheses

Anonymous
From the Sacred Harp, 1844
arr. by William Bay

Fingerstyle Guitar Acc.

Moderately ♩ = 90

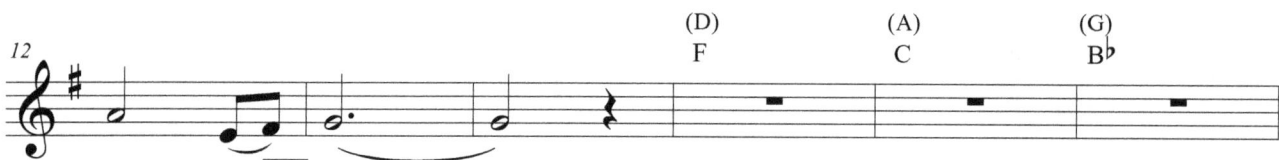

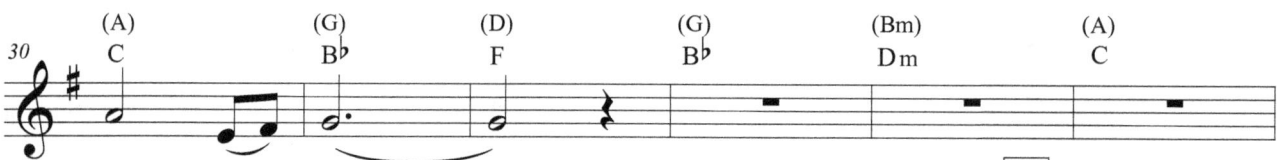

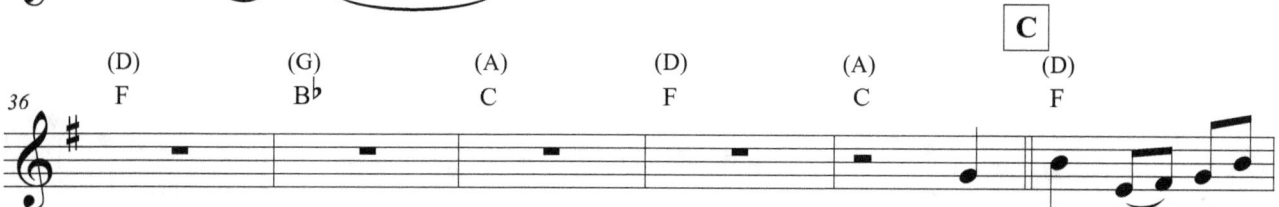

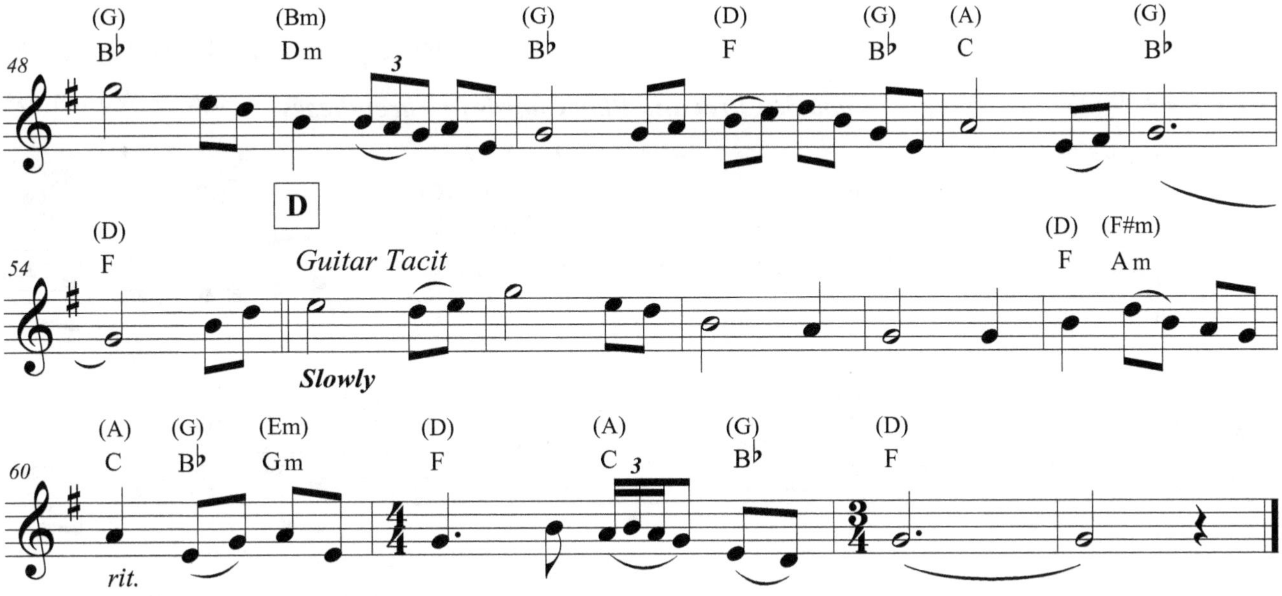
(G) B♭ (Bm) Dm (G) B♭ (D) F (G) B♭ (A) C (G) B♭
D
(D) F
Guitar Tacit
Slowly
(D) F (F#m) Am
(A) C (G) B♭ (Em) Gm (D) F (A) C (G) B♭ (D) F
rit.

Come, Thou Fount of Every Blessing
Nettleton

Wyeth's Repository of Sacred Music, 1813

Guitar: Capo 3rd Fret and Play Chords in Parentheses

arr. by William Bay

Lively ♩ = 100

42
(G7) B♭7
(F) A♭
(G7) B♭7
(C) E♭
(G7) B♭7
(C) E♭
(G) B♭
46
(F) A♭
(C) E♭
(G7) B♭7
(C) E♭
(G7) B♭7
rit.
(C) E♭
(F) A♭
(G) B♭
50
(C) E♭
(F) A♭
(C) E♭
(G) B♭
(G7) B♭7
3
(C) E♭

Come, Thou Almighty King
Italian Hymn

Fingerstyle or Strum Guitar Acc.

Felice de Giardini
arr. by William Bay

Moderato ♩ = 128

Come, Ye Disconsolate
Consolator

Fingerstyle or Strum Guitar Acc.

Samuel Webbe

arr. by William Bay

Come, Ye Thankful People, Come
St. George's Windsor

Strum Guitar Acc.

George. J. Elvey
arr. by William Bay

Boldly ♩ = 106

Crown Him with Many Crowns
Diademata

Strum Guitar Acc.

George J. Elvey

arr. by William Bay

Triumphantly ♩ = 100

Dear Lord and Father of Mankind
Repton

Guitar: Capo 3rd Fret and Play Chords in Parentheses

Fingerstyle Guitar Acc.

Charles Hubert Hastings Parry

arr. by William Bay

Doxology
Old 100th

Guitar: Capo 3rd Fret and Play Chords in Parentheses

Fingerstyle or Strum Guitar Acc.

Louis Bourgeois

arr. by William Bay

Fairest Lord Jesus
St. Elizabeth

Guitar: Capo 3rd Fret and Play Chords in Parentheses

Fingerstyle Guitar Acc.

Anonymous
arr. by William Bay

Lyrically ♩ = 94

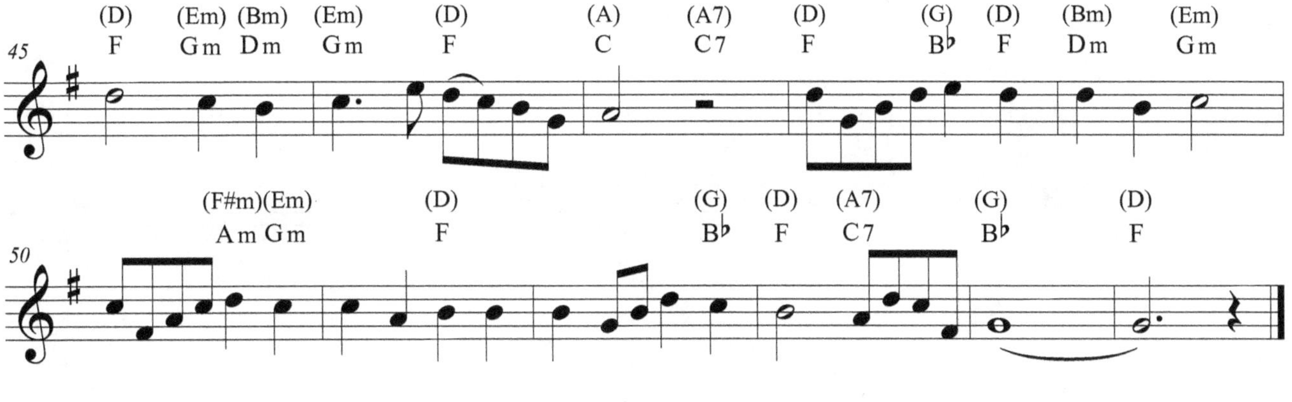
(D) (Em) (Bm) (Em) (D) (A) (A7) (D) (G) (D) (Bm) (Em)
F Gm Dm Gm F C C7 F B♭ F Dm Gm
45
(F#m)(Em) (D) (G) (D) (A7) (G) (D)
Am Gm F B♭ F C7 B♭ F
50

Faith of Our Fathers
St. Catherine

Fingerstyle Guitar Acc.

Henri F. Hemy
arr. by William Bay

Lyrically ♩ = 106

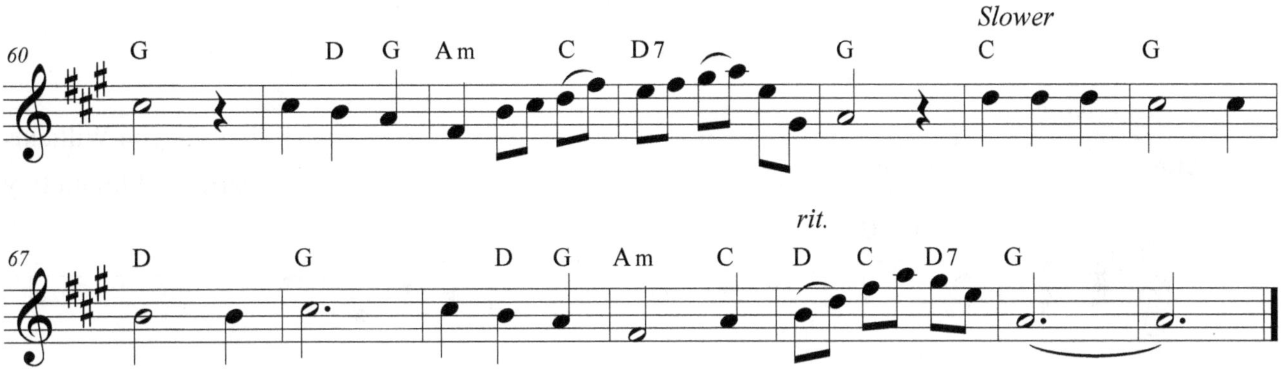
Slower
60
G D G Am C D7 G C G
rit.
67
D G D G Am C D C D7 G

For All the Saints
Sine Nomine

Strum Guitar Acc.

Allegro ♩ = 136

Ralph Vaughn Williams
arr. by William Bay

For the Beauty of the Earth
Dix

Fingerstyle Guitar Acc.

Conrad Kocher
arr. by William Bay

Moderato ♩ = 90

Glorious Things of Thee Are Spoken
Austrian Hymn

Guitar: Capo 3rd Fret and Play Chords in Parentheses

Strum or Fingerstyle Guitar Acc.

Franz Joseph Haydn
arr. by William Bay

Moderately ♩ = 100

Glory Be to Jesus
Caswall

Moderately ♩ = 84   ***Guitar: Capo 3rd Fret and Play Chords in Parentheses***   Friedrich Filitz, 1847
arr. by William Bay

Fingerstyle Guitar Acc.

Guide Me, O Thou Great Jehovah
CWM Rhondda

John Hughes
arr. by William Bay

Strum Guitar Acc.

Hail the Day that Sees Him Rise
Llanfair

Guitar: Capo 3rd Fret and Play Chords in Parentheses

Robert Williams
arr. by William Bay

Fingerstyle or Strum Guitar Acc.

He is Risen
Unser Herrsher

Strum Guitar Acc.

Joachim Neander

arr. by William Bay

Here, O My Lord
Penitentia

Fingerstyle Guitar Acc.

Edward Dearle

Guitar: Capo 3rd Fret and Play Chords in Parentheses arr. by William Bay

Holy God, We Praise Your Name
Grosser Gott

Fingerstyle Guitar Acc.

Katholisches Gesanbuch
arr. by William Bay

Holy, Holy, Holy
Nicaea

John B. Dykes, 1861
arr. by William Bay

Strum Guitar Acc.

Guitar: Capo 3rd Fret and Play Chords in Parentheses

Hosanna, Loud Hosanna
Ellacombe

Strum Guitar Acc.

Guitar: Capo 3rd Fret and Play Chords in Parentheses

Gesanbuch der Herzogl
arr. by William Bay

Moderato ♩ = 120

This page has been left blank to avoid an awkward page turn

How Sweet the Name of Jesus Sounds
St. Peter

Fingerstyle Guitar Acc.

Alexander R. Reinagle

arr. by William Bay

Moderato ♩ = 98

I Love Thy Kingdom, Lord
St. Thomas

Strum Guitar Acc.

Aaron Williams

arr. by William Bay

59

I Want to Walk as a Child of the Light
Houston
Guitar: Capo 3rd fret and Play Chords in Parentheses

Fingerstyle Guitar Acc.

Kathleen Thomerson
arr. by William Bay

Lyrically ♩ = 106

49
(C) (F) (Em) (G) (C) (G) (F) (C) (Dm)
E♭ A♭ Gm B♭ E♭ B♭ A♭ E♭ Fm
54
(Em) (C) (F) (C) (F) (Em) (Am) (C) (Dm) (C) (G)
Gm E♭ A♭ E♭ A♭ Gm Cm E♭ Fm E♭ B♭
D
59
(F) (G) (C) (G) (F) (Em) (C) (F)
A♭ B♭ E♭ B♭ A♭ Gm E♭ A♭
64
(Em) (C) (G) (F) (C) (G) (Am) (D) (G)
Gm E♭ B♭ A♭ E♭ B♭ Cm F B♭
69
(Am) (Em) (Am) (Em) (F) (G)
Cm Gm Cm Gm A♭ B♭
74
(C) (G) (Em) (G) (C)
E♭ B♭ Gm B♭ E♭
rit.
78
(F) (C)
A♭ E♭

I Will Arise and Go to Jesus
Arise/Restoration

Guitar: Capo 1st Fret and Play Chords in Parentheses

Fingerstyle Guitar Acc.

Anonymous
Southern Harmony, 1835
arr. by William Bay

Gently ♩ = 84

62

Immortal, Invisible, God Only Wise
St. Denio

Strum Guitar Acc.

Caniadau y Cyssegr

arr. by William Bay

In the Cross of Christ I Glory
Rathbun

Fingerstyle or Strum Guitar Acc.

Ithamar Conkey
arr. by William Bay

This page has been left blank to avoid an awkward page turn

It is Well with My Soul
Ville Du Havre

Fingerstyle Guitar Acc.

Philip P. Bliss 1838-1876

arr. by William Bay

Lyrically ♩ = 92

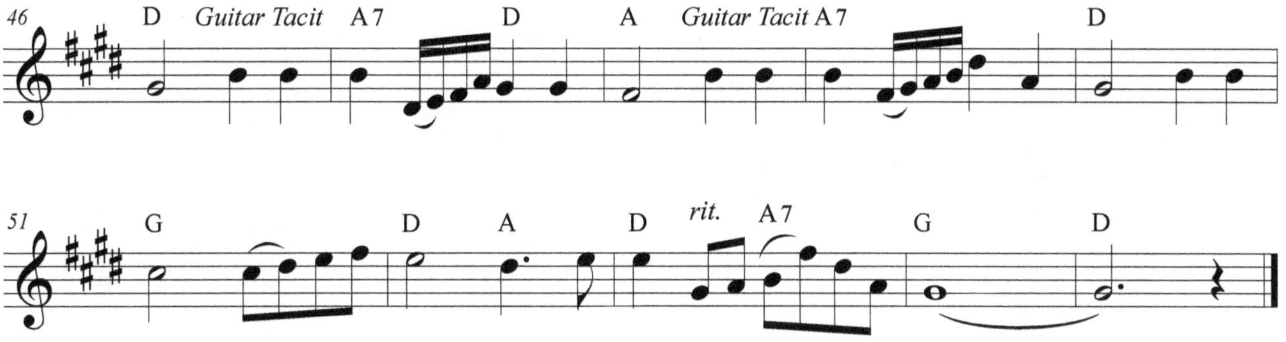
46
D
Guitar Tacit
A7
D
A
Guitar Tacit
A7
D
51
G
D
A
D
rit.
A7
G
D

Jesus Calls Us
Pleading Savior

Guitar: Capo 3rd Fret and Play Chords in Parentheses

Fingerstyle or Strum Guitar Acc.

Early American Hymn
arr. by William Bay

D
(G) B♭ (D) F (A7) C7 (D) F (F#m) Am (Bm) Dm (Em) Gm (D) F
73
(F#m) Am (Bm) Dm (F#m) Am (A7) C7 (D) F (G) B♭ (D) F (A7) C7
3
81
(D) F (G) B♭ (D) F (Bm) Dm (A7) C7 (D) F (A) C (A7) C7 (D) F (G) B♭
91
(F#m) Am (A) C (D) F (G) B♭ (D) F (Bm) Dm (A) C (A7) C7
99
(D) F (G) B♭ (D) F

Jesus Shall Reign
Duke Street

Joyful, Joyful, We Adore Thee
Hymn to Joy

Strum Guitar Acc.

Ludwig van Beethoven
arr. by William Bay

Boldly ♩ = 114

71

Land of Rest
Often Sung As "Jerusalem, My Happy Home"

Fingerstyle Guitar Acc.

Early American Melody
arr. by William Bay

Allegro ♩ = 140

57
Bm C D D7 G C Bm
E
64
E7 A C♯m7 F♯m E A Bm7
71
G E F♯m C♯m7 F♯m A F♯m
78
Bm E F♯m E A D
rit.
a tempo
83
E D A E A

Let All Mortal Flesh Keep Silence
Picardy

Guitar: Capo 1st Fret and Play Chords in Parentheses

Fingerstyle Guitar Acc.

Traditional French
arr. by William Bay

Gently ♩ = 74

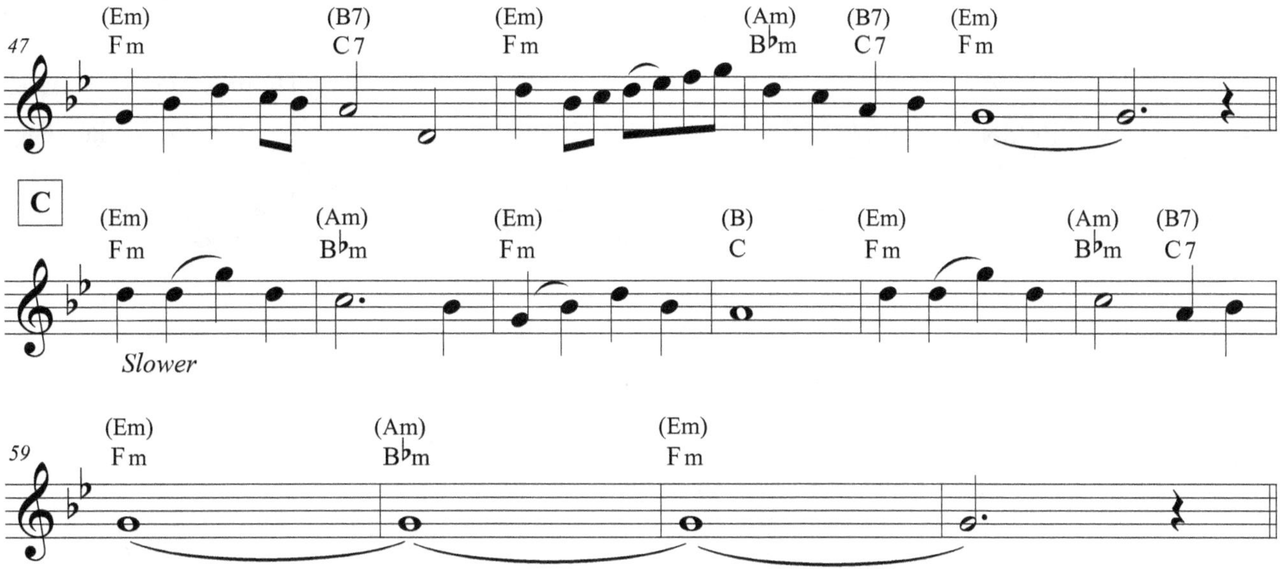
47
(Em) Fm
(B7) C7
(Em) Fm
(Am) B♭m
(B7) C7
(Em) Fm
C
(Em) Fm
(Am) B♭m
(Em) Fm
(B) C
(Em) Fm
(Am) B♭m
(B7) C7
Slower
59
(Em) Fm
(Am) B♭m
(Em) Fm

Lo! He Comes, with Clouds Descending
Helmsley

Strum Guitar Acc.

Thomas Augustine Arne
arr. by William Bay

Boldly ♩ = 132

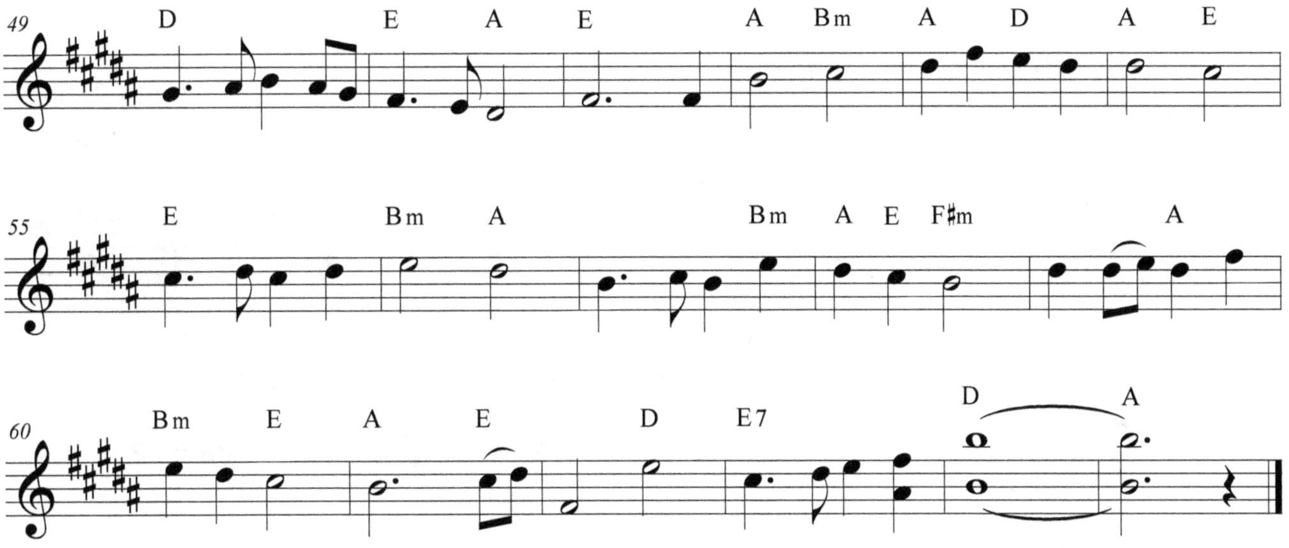
49
D E A E A Bm A D A E
55
E Bm A Bm A E F♯m A
60
Bm E A E D E7 D A

Lead On, O King Eternal
Lancashire

Fingerstyle or Strum Guitar Acc.

Henry T. Smart
arr. by William Bay

Moderately ♩ = 106

Lord, Speak to Me
Canonbury

Fingerstyle Guitar Acc.

Robert Schumann
arr. by William Bay

Love Divine
Beecher

Guitar: Capo 3rd Fret and Play Chords in Parentheses

Fingerstyle Guitar Acc.

John Zundel
arr. by William Bay

Moderato ♩ = 100

My Hope is Built on Nothing Less
Solid Rock

Fingerstyle or Strum Guitar Acc.

William Bradbury
arr. by William Bay

Moderato ♩ = 106

My Jesus, I Love Thee
Gordon

Fingerstyle Guitar Acc.

Adoniram J. Gordon

arr. by William Bay

Lyrically ♩ = 92

Now Thank We All Our God
Nun Danket

Guitar: Capo 3rd Fret and Play Chords in Parentheses

Johann Crüger
arr. by William Bay

Strum or Fingerstyle Guitar Acc.

O God, We Praise Thee
Morning Song

Guitar: Capo 3rd Fret and Play Chords in Parentheses

Fingerstyle Guitar Acc.

Anonymous
Wyeth's Repository of Sacred Music, 1813

arr. by William Bay

Gently ♩ = 82

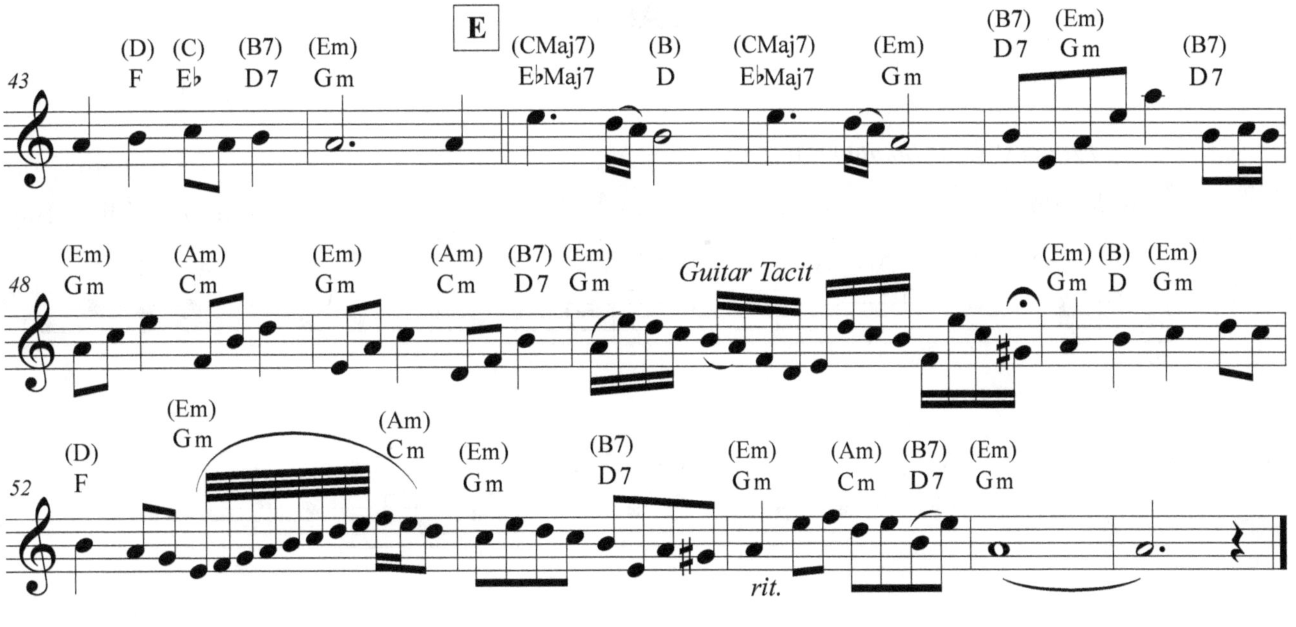
43
(D) F
(C) E♭
(B7) D7
(Em) Gm
E
(CMaj7) E♭Maj7
(B) D
(CMaj7) E♭Maj7
(Em) Gm
(B7) D7
(Em) Gm
(B7) D7
48
(Em) Gm
(Am) Cm
(Em) Gm
(Am) Cm
(B7) D7
(Em) Gm
Guitar Tacit
(Em) Gm
(B) D
(Em) Gm
52
(D) F
(Em) Gm
(Am) Cm
(Em) Gm
(B7) D7
(Em) Gm
(Am) Cm
(B7) D7
(Em) Gm
rit.

O God, Our Help in Ages Past
St. Anne

Fingerstyle or Strum Guitar Acc.

William Croft
arr. by William Bay

Moderato ♩ = 104

O Master, Let Me Walk with Thee
Maryton

Guitar: Capo 3rd Fret and Play Chords in Parentheses

Fingerstyle Guitar Acc.

H. Percy Smith

arr. by William Bay

O Praise Ye the Lord!
Laudate Dominum

Guitar: Capo 1st Fret and Play Chords in Parentheses

Charles Hubert Hastings Parry

arr. by William Bay

Fingerstyle or Strum Gtr. Acc.

O Sacred Head, Now Wounded
Herzlich Tut Mich Verlangen

Fingerstyle Guitar Accompaniment

J.S. Bach
arr. by William Bay

O Savior, Rend the Heavens Wide
O Heiland, Reiss Die Himmel Auf

Gesangbuch, Augsburg, 1666
arr. by William Bay

Strum Guitar Acc.

Boldly ♩ = 100

O Worship the King
Lyons

Guitar: Capo 3rd Fret and Play Chords in Parentheses   Johann Michael Haydn

Fingerstyle or Strum Guitar Acc.   arr. by William Bay

91

Oh, For a Thousand Tongues to Sing
Azmon

Strum Guitar Acc.

Lowell Mason
arr. by William Bay

Moderato ♩ = 112

92

Oh, the Deep, Deep Love of Jesus
Ebenezer

Guitar: Capo 1st Fret and Play Chords in Parentheses

Fingerstyle or Strum Guitar Acc.

Thomas J. Williams
arr. by William Bay

Praise My Soul, the King of Heaven
Lauda Anima

Fingerstyle or Strum Guitar Acc.

John Goss, 1869
arr. by William Bay

Boldly ♩ = 96

49
A7
Bm
D
Em
A
E7
55
A
A7
E
E7
A
Bm
A
G
D
61
Bm
Em
A
G
D
Em
D
A7
D
C
D
G
A
D
G
D
rit.
72
Em
A7
Bm
A7
D

Praise to the Lord, the Almighty
Lobe den Herren

Strum Guitar Acc.

Joachim Neander
arr. by William Bay

Boldly ♩ = 110

Rejoice, O Pure in Heart
Marion

Strum Guitar Acc.

Arthur H. Messiter
arr. by William Bay

Moderato ♩ = 116

Rejoice, the Lord is King
Darwall

Guitar: Capo 3rd Fret and Play Chords in Parentheses

Strum Guitar Acc.

John Darwall

arr. by William Bay

Boldly ♩ = 110

Shall We Gather at the River/Alternate Melody
Palmetto

Fingerstyle Guitar Acc.

Anonymous
arr. by William Bay

Adagio ♩ = 66

99

Sing Praise to God Who Reigns Above
Mit Freuden Zart

Strum Guitar Acc.

Bohemian Brethren's Kirchengesänge
arr. by William Bay

Moderato ♩ = 98

Spirit of God, Descend upon My Heart
Morecambe

Fingerstyle Guitar Acc.

Frederick C. Atkinson

arr. by William Bay

Thaxted
Sung as "O God Beyond All Praising"

Fingerstyle Guitar Acc.

Gustav Holst/From "The Planets"

arr. by William Bay

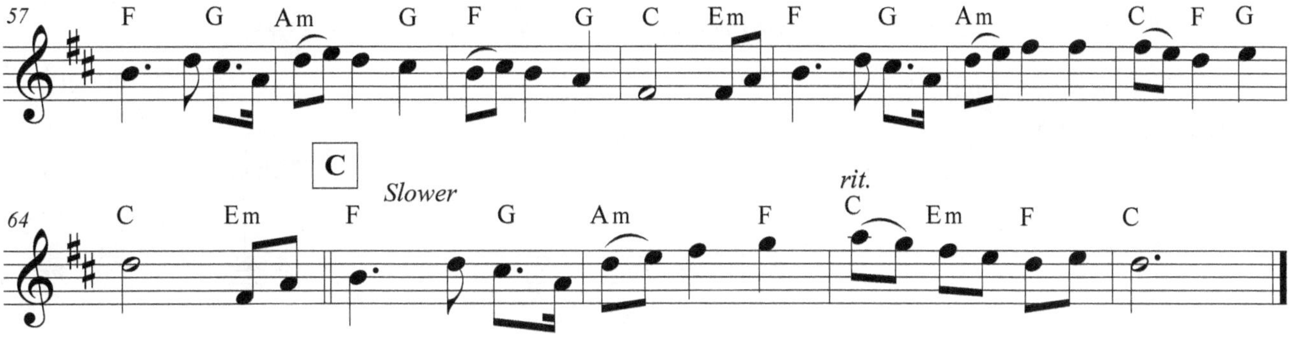
57
F G Am G F G C Em F G Am C F G
C
Slower
rit.
64
C Em F G Am F C Em F C

Star of the County Down
Sung As "The Mighty God with Power Speaks"

Guitar: Capo 3rd Fret and Play Chords in Parentheses

Traditional Irish
arr. by William Bay

The Church's One Foundation
Aurelia

Guitar: Capo 3rd Fret and Play Chords in Parentheses

Fingerstyle Guitar Acc.

Samuel Wesley
arr. by William Bay

The God of Abraham Praise
Leoni

Guitar: Capo 1st Fret and Play Chords in Parentheses

Meyer Lyon
arr. by William Bay

Fingerstyle Guitar Acc.

Moderately ♩ = 108

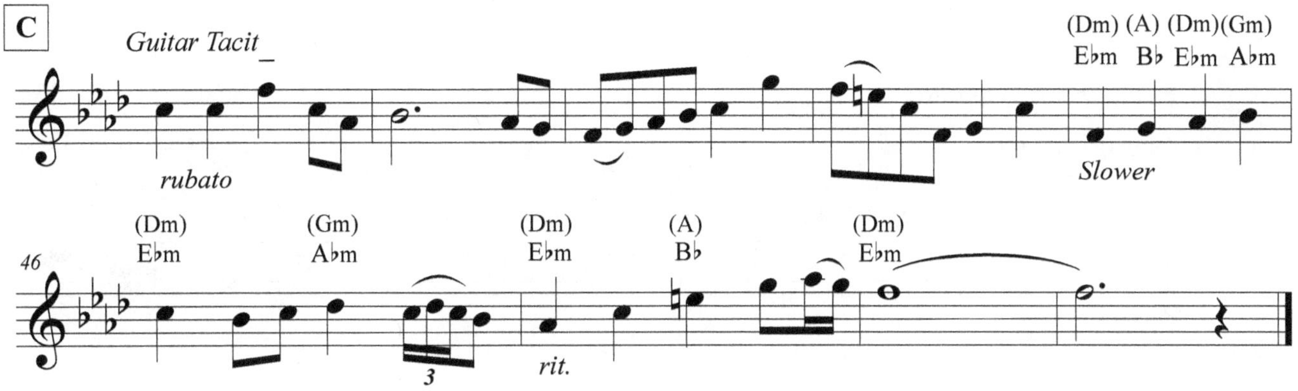
C
Guitar Tacit
rubato
(Dm) (A) (Dm)(Gm)
E♭m B♭ E♭m A♭m
Slower
46
(Dm) E♭m
(Gm) A♭m
3
(Dm) E♭m
rit.
(A) B♭
(Dm) E♭m

The Day is Past and Gone
Evening Shade

Anonymous
Sacred Harp, 1835
arr. by William Bay

Fingerstyle Guitar Acc.

Moderato ♩ = 120

The King of Love My Shepherd Is
St. Columba

Guitar: Capo 3rd Fret and Play Chords in Parentheses

Fingerstyle Guitar Acc.

Traditional Irish
arr. by William Bay

Lyrically ♩ = 90

The Lord is My Shepherd
Brother James' Air

Fingerstyle or Strum Guitar Acc.

J.L. Macbeth Bain

arr. by William Bay

Gently ♩ = 94

The Lord Our God is Clothed with Might
Detroit

Guitar: Capo 1st Fret and Play Chords in Parentheses

Fingerstyle Guitar Acc.

Kentucky Harmony, 1820
arr. by William Bay

Moderately ♩ = 102

The Lord's Supper
Way

Guitar: Capo 3rd Fret and Play Chords in Parentheses

Fingerstyle Guitar Acc.

William Bay

(Em) (Bm) (D) (Em) (B7) (Em) (Am) (Em)
Gm Dm F Gm D7 Gm Cm Gm
D
(Am) (B7) (Am) (B7) (Em) (Am) (Em) (B7)
Cm D7 Cm D7 Gm Cm Gm D7
(Em) (Am) (B7) (Em) (B7) (Em)
Gm Cm D7 Gm D7 Gm
rit.
(B7) (Em) (Bm) (Em) (Bm) (Em)
D7 Gm Dm Gm Dm Gm
dim.

The Spacious Firmament on High
Creation

Fingerstyle or Strum Guitar Acc.

Franz J. Haydn
arr. by William Bay

Moderato ♩ = 82

51
Bm A E7 A E A E A D A E
57
E7 Bm A E7 A E A
63
E A E A E A E
69
A E A E A Bm
More Slowly
75
A E7 A E A Bm A E7 A

The Lord's My Shepherd
Crimond

Guitar: Capo 3rd Fret and Play Chords in Parentheses

Fingerstyle Guitar Acc.

Jessie Seymour Irvine
arr. by William Bay

116

The Strife is O'er, the Battle Done
Victory

Strum or Fingerstyle Guitar Acc.

Giovanni da Palestrina, 1591

arr. by William Bay

Boldly ♩ = 134

The Wedding Feast of Cana
Ag an bPósadh Bhi i gCána

Guitar: Capo 3rd Fret and Play Chords in Parentheses

Fingerstyle or Strum Guitar Acc.

Traditional Irish
arr. by William Bay

Andante ♩ = 78

This is My Father's World
Terra Beata

Fingerstyle Guitar Acc.

Franklin L. Sheppard
arr. by William Bay

Moderato ♩ = 98

Thine is the Glory
Judas Maccabaeus

Guitar: Capo 3rd Fret and Play Chords in Parentheses

G. F. Handel

arr. by William Bay

Moderately ♩ = 108

Strum Guitar Acc.

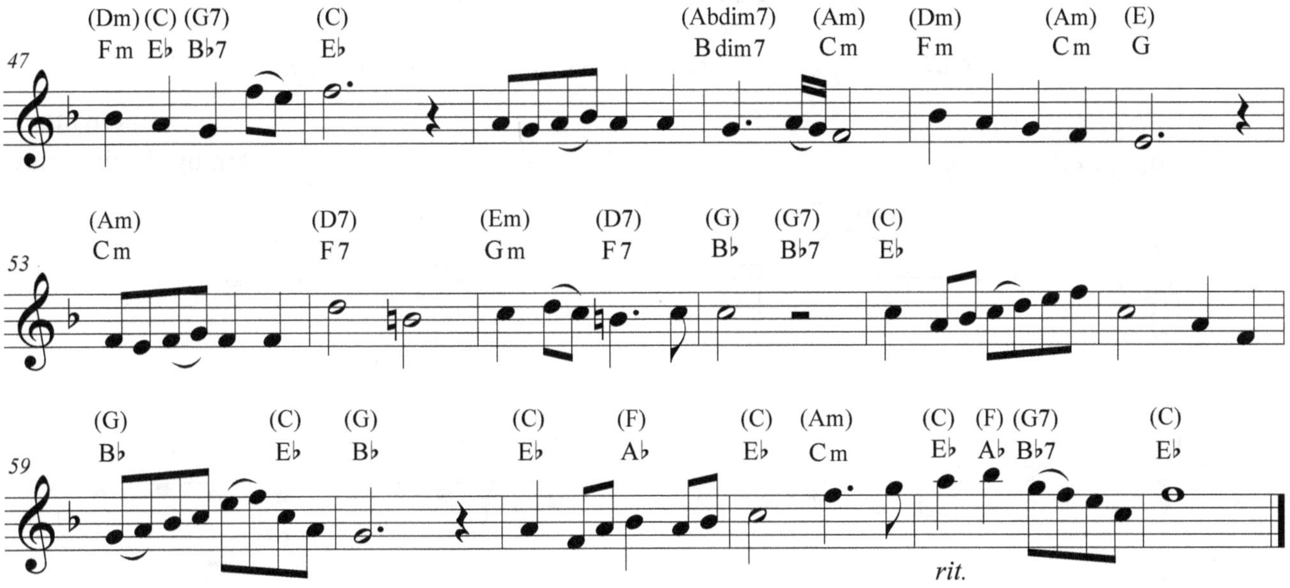
47
(Dm) (C) (G7) (C) (Abdim7) (Am) (Dm) (Am) (E)
Fm E♭ B♭7 E♭ B dim7 Cm Fm Cm G
53
(Am) (D7) (Em) (D7) (G) (G7) (C)
Cm F7 Gm F7 B♭ B♭7 E♭
59
(G) (C) (G) (C) (F) (C) (Am) (C) (F) (G7) (C)
B♭ E♭ B♭ E♭ A♭ E♭ Cm E♭ A♭ B♭7 E♭
rit.

Veni Redemptor gentium
Plainsong, 12th Century

Guitar: Capo 1st Fret and Play Chords in Parentheses

Fingerstyle Guitar Acc.

Anonymous
arr. by William Bay

Gently ♩ = 86

123

Watchman, Tell Us of the Night
Aberystwyth

Fingerstyle Guitar Acc.

Joseph Parry
arr. by William Bay

Wayfarin' Stranger

Guitar: Capo 1st Fret and Play Chords in Parentheses

Traditional Spiritual
arr. by William Bay

Fingerstyle or Strum Guitar Acc.

Slowly ♩ = 76

We Gather Together
Kremser

Guitar: Capo 3rd Fret and Play Chords in Parentheses

Fingerstyle Guitar Acc.

Nederlandtsch Gedenckclank, 1626
arr. by William Bay

Lyrically ♩ = 98

126

Were You There?

Guitar: Capo 3rd Fret and Play Chords in Parentheses

Fingerstyle Guitar Acc.

Traditional Spiritual

arr. by William Bay

Andante ♩ = 74

127

When Jesus Left His Father's Throne
Kingsfold

Guitar: Capo 1st Fret and Play Chords in Parentheses

Traditional English
arr. by William Bay

Fingerstlyle or Strum Guitar Acc.

Majestically ♩ = 104

128

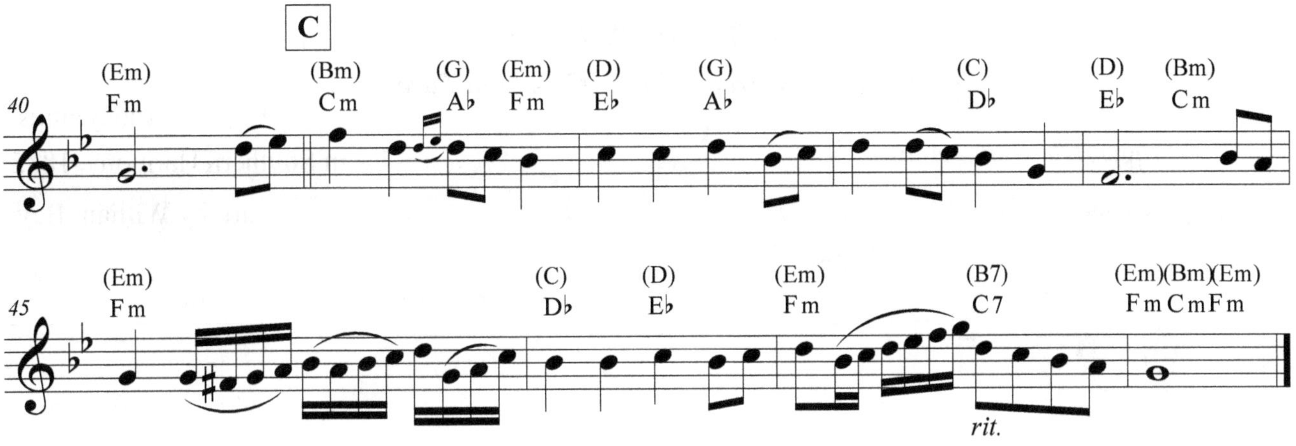
C
(Em) (Bm) (G) (Em) (D) (G) (C) (D) (Bm)
Fm Cm A♭ Fm E♭ A♭ D♭ E♭ Cm
40
(Em) (C) (D) (Em) (B7) (Em)(Bm)(Em)
Fm D♭ E♭ Fm C7 Fm Cm Fm
45
rit.

What Wondrous Love
Wondrous Love
Guitar: Capo 3rd Fret and Play Chords in Parentheses

Anonymous
From Southern Harmony, 1835
arr. by William Bay

Fingerstyle Guitar Acc.

Moderately ♩ = 96

130

48
(G) (Am) (G) (Em) (FMaJ7) (Em) (Dm) (Am) (G) (Am)
B♭ Cm B♭ Gm A♭Maj7 Gm Fm Cm B♭ Cm
C
53
(F) (Dm) (F) (Em) (G) (C) (F) (Em) (Am) (G)
A♭ Fm A♭ Gm B♭ E♭ A♭ Gm Cm B♭
3
59
(Am) (G) (Em) (Am) (Dm) (FMaj7) (Em) (G) (Am)
Cm B♭ Gm Cm Fm A♭Maj7 Gm B♭ Cm
rit.
65
(G) (Am) (Em) (F) (Am) (FMaj7) (Am)
B♭ Cm Gm A♭ Cm A♭Maj7 Cm

When I Survey the Wondrous Cross
Rockingham

Fingerstlyle or Strum Guitar Acc.

Isaac Watts

arr. by William Bay

Moderately ♩ = 110

www.ingramcontent.com/pod-product-compliance
Lightning Source LLC
Chambersburg PA
CBHW081427090426
42740CB00017B/3206

9780998384252